KELLY PRICE NOBLE, DHA

Blessed with Activity™

A Mindfulness Journey

AuthorHouse™
1663 Liberty Drive
Bloomington, IN 47403
www.authorhouse.com
Phone: 1 (800) 839-8640

Published by AuthorHouse 07/24/2018

ISBN: 978-1-5462-5126-2 (sc)
ISBN: 978-1-5462-5127-9 (hc)
ISBN: 978-1-5462-5125-5 (e)

Library of Congress Control Number: 2018908306

Print information available on the last page.

Blessed with Activity™:
A Mindfulness Journey

Kelly Price Noble, DHA

2018

Dedication

To all who believed in me, even when you thought I was crazily insane to pick up yet another project! I love you!

Table of Contents

Foreword

How often do we get caught up in our everyday lives? Running to get the children to school, stopping to get coffee before our 9 AM meeting; then off to this practice, that school function, or another evening meeting. How often do we hear ourselves or others say, "if only I had more time to…"? Instead of getting upset about what we are doing shouldn't we be thankful we have activities to attend or places to go?

I remember the first-time meeting Dr. Noble; she was the Faculty Liaison for Delta Mu Delta International Honor Society of Business at the University of Phoenix, San Diego Campus. I was just going into my second-year residency for my doctorate in Organizational Leadership. I asked her how she was. She replied, "*Blessed with Activity*!" The statement caught me off guard. I was expecting, "fine," "great," or "wonderful" but "*Blessed with Activity*." Not my first comeback.

As I got to know Dr. Kelly, as I affectionately call her, that was her tag line, "Blessed with Activity!" Whenever I or someone else asked how she was doing, she always replied, "*Blessed with Activity!*"

Dr. Kelly had two children in college on opposite sides of the country. She drove to Los Angeles, working with Reboot, helped females transition from the military to civilian life, taught in the evenings at least twice a week, and was involved with countless other activities. Yet, she always had a smile on her face, was positive, and more concerned with helping others than talking about what she was doing or complaining.

There will always be meetings, school functions, sporting events, or something needing our attention. We could look at these activities from the negative side: getting up early for meetings, earlier to get the children to school, staying out late because of school functions or even later with sporting events. Or, we could look at these activities as a blessing: spending time with our families, sharing our talents with our co-workers, cheering on your child's friend because his or her parents could not make the sporting event.

You've heard the saying, "when life sends you lemons, make lemonade!" Well, that's what these passages do; they help you make lemonade! Anyone who feeling overwhelmed from school, parenting, work, or life in general will find comfort and healing through "Minnie's Pearls," "See Obstacles as Opportunities," "Your Turn to do the Dishes," or even "Quilting," yes, "Quilting!"

As I read these passages, I realized these were the same golden nuggets she would tell me, as she helped me through my doctoral journey. A time of self-doubt, low self-esteem, and lacking confidence. The writings are more than words on paper; they are golden nuggets of wisdom anyone can apply to his or her life, as they did to help overcome my struggles.

We can be negative in our activities, making everyone around us miserable, or we can be positive, choosing to be *Blessed with Activity*!"

Dr. Lynda K. Majerowicz

Author's Preface

"God would not give me anything I couldn't handle! I just wish he didn't trust me so much!"

~Mother Teresa

Years ago, I was blessed to have worked with Spinal Cord Injured Veterans; many of whom became dear friends. I can't even tell you how long ago, perhaps 2005. I worked and travelled with them for eight years. I loved my job, so much so I even based my doctoral dissertation on a significant group: *Identifying Quality Long-term Care for Non-Service-Connected Spinal Cord Injured Veterans: Isolating Barriers to Care.*

Every March, Veteran Service Organizations (VSO), from around the country, would descend upon Washington, D. C., to testify in front of the Joint Hearing Committee, seeking to improve benefits for veterans and their families. I had the privilege to attend those meetings, as well as convene with our State Representatives. The movement was powerful. Members of VSOs, staff, and families arrived en force in wheelchairs, walkers prepared to fight for rights service members were promised when they took the oath to "support and defend the Constitution of the United States" (U. S. Army Center of Military History, n. d., para. 1).

I quickly discovered, I was blessed each day to rise by myself without the aid of an attendant, knowing activities of daily life were under my control. Humbled, I observed how veterans (and others) manage with spinal cord dysfunctions. You think your day is tough? Wait until your mode of getting around changes, completely.

Have you ever been carried on to a plane, so whimsically you thought someone might drop you? Did earning your college degree take six years, because classes you needed were on the second floor, and no elevator was available to get you there?

So, when people asked me how are you doing? My go to response was, "I got up." I ran the halls of the hospital, meetings, events, and even waited for port-a-potties in the wee hours of the morning. All, because I could. Friends and colleagues would say, "I just want to follow you one day. You are always on the go. Do you ever sleep?"

"Yes", I would say. But, when I go down, I go down like a felled tree." My boss once called me the Tasmanian Devil! Ha!!

A mother, wife, daughter, sister, aunt, niece, full-time employee, volunteer, professor, gardener, quilter, exerciser, and student, I was, and still am, *Blessed with Activity*. As long as I am able, I will move, jump, act a goof.

Always in motion, like an atomic mass: working in VA Spinal Cord Center, finishing my Masters, teaching, rearing two young, athletic children, marrying my best friend, creating events, volunteering, ... I remained grateful for the activity for which I was given. I know few people complain about their busy schedules, but to me, I wanted to be a part of each day, give to each day. While on the treadmill, one afternoon, I listened to Stephen Covey's 1989 book, *Seven Habits of Highly Effective People*. Below are a few quotes I've taken and apply to life. Some need a little more practice than others.

1. **Companies have missions; you should, too.**
2. **"There are three constants in life... change, choice and principles" (Brainyquotes, n. d.a, para. 1).**
3. **"The key is not to prioritize what's on your schedule, but to schedule your priorities" (Brainyquotes, n. d.b, section 1).**

Each activity was my choice. I rarely do anything I do not want to. As long as people knew my family came first that was all that mattered. Sometimes, others would sprinkle a few extra things on my to do list. I did not complain for the alternative may have been boredom. And, for heaven's sake, you would not want me bored. I was that kid who looked in your cabinets!

I was that kid who refused to come inside, no matter how badly I had to go to the bathroom. I walked into a field of cacti just to see how far I could get only to have a parent rescue me 'cause I went too far. As an adult, I was Homecoming Chair at my kids' school, my husband and I had the bright idea to bring in classic cars for the Homecoming Court Procession. Well, I had to drive one of them. One year, I drove our 1966 Corvette. You see, I had to get my part of the Court to their places on the field then "race" back to be in line, as a Senior Football Player's Mom for my son to present me with a rose!

That same year, my son, the Receiver, caught the ball and ran 90 yards for a touchdown! I heard the crowd cheering for someone and realized my son had the ball. So, what does any mother do? She runs her fastest to see the play. What Else? I ran up the sideline to meet him, pacing him down to the end zone. Not only was sideline footage captured of the event, an enfield camera captured it as well. Great for Monday afternoon huddle.

Well, you will find more inside. Thanks to my family and their patience, I've begun another project. This one with their blessings.

Acknowledgments

Ron, Rachael, Nathaniel, Mother, Daddy, Laura, Keirre, Lynda, and Art

Prologue

Blessed with Activity, yes, true my mantra, became a reality when I would respond to people asking, how are you? "Blessed with Activity." A few times, when responding, I felt some would shy away if I said Blessed versus lucky or fortunate. But, these were/are my words and how I feel. They are not necessarily meant to be religious in aspect but to be something for which I am most grateful. I am busy all the time. Truly never bored. My choice.

After a while of me saying, Blessed with Activity, People would respond with, I'm going to use that! It explains my life! So many people said this to me, I felt, I've got to do something about this. So, I did. BLESSED WITH ACTIVITY™

I've created apparel and accessories; I'm introducing and now you are reading my book. Please visit www.BlessedwithActivity.com for more options. Join my email list.

Demographics for me are widespread. What I did not realize was I missed one: retired seniors. I met a SCORE (Senior Counselors of Retired Executives) Mentor who said he had so much activity when he was working. When he retired, he noted he didn't know what he had while he was working. Since our initial meeting, he's been thinking about Blessed with Activity!

Blessed with Activity™

◇◇◇

Every day, when I rise, my choice is to be part of the day. Starting from my cup of coffee, letting the dogs out (and then in, again), surveying my garden, talking to each bud reaching for the sky. I'm grateful to have such activity.

When I began this "campaign", if you will, it was just a saying, something I shared willingly with others. Then, it became a "thing", a movement. Once I explained my rationale behind Blessed with Activity, people got it!

Think about "it" for a moment. This saying is not necessarily religious, but it sure is powerful. The slogan can be applied to busy parents, working adults, athletes, and camp counselors chasing kids around the yard. Then I was presented with a different demographic, the Retiree. Blessed with activity while he or she worked for years on end, waiting for "that day" when someone said, "You are retired!" Ok, now what?

Well, after having been so busy for years, retirees began to miss the action of engaging with people on a frequent basis. Some so much so, they have been able to adjust to a sedentary lifestyle. Not everyone wants to play golf. That's a whole other story.

The grass looks greener on the other side, doesn't it? Be blessed with the activity you have been given. Do not complain you have so much to do. Ponder this gift, for the opportunity of wholeness could be right around the corner.

Me

◇◇◇◇◇◇◇

Born at Wright Patterson Air Force base, my father, Kline A. Price, Jr., said I was the loudest baby in the Nursery. Well, of course I was. My mother, Bebe Drew Price, was in labor with me for three days. Wouldn't you be screaming, too?

When I was little, my parents would say, she doesn't want to miss a thing. They would watch through the kitchen window, as I'd cross my legs, trying to hold back the urine. Yes, urine. We didn't say pee in our house. Lurinate was what I said until I knew better.

Mother and Daddy gave us everything we needed. They encouraged us (I am the eldest of four) to play, run, and jump. Getting dirty was okay. Mother said, "We have a washing machine!"

One day, I guess I played so hard, I literally stopped in my tracks, falling asleep right where I fell ...in the toy box. My parents were frantic. Then they heard subtle sounds of a snor. To this day, I will bop til I drop; the drop, however, may be preceded by the flame out, then the spiral, and "she's out!"

The Road Not Taken

◇◇◇◇◇◇◇◇◇◇◇◇◇◇◇◇◇◇◇◇◇◇◇◇◇◇◇◇◇◇◇◇◇◇◇◇

Robert Frost's Poem, A Road Not Taken, has been my favorite since 7th grade graduation. Little did I know then is when I do something, I go all the way. I like to make footprints in the snow. I like to try new things or test boundaries. Many reading this, who know me, are probably shaking their heads.

I will follow someone if I know he or she is heading in the correct direction or doing something smart. When traveling with Wall $treet Week with Louis Rukeyser production team to London, England, our Producer was stopped by

Customs. He was grimy-looking with newspaper ink over his hands and Oreo cookies on his lips; the rest of us were pulled in, too. Lesson learned. Be clean and polite when going through Customs.

See?! I diverged.

One of the many reasons I drive a Suburban is I want to know what is ahead of me. And, if need be, I want time to go around. Never know when that 18-wheeler ahead of you is going to stop. Seeing 15 cars ahead gives time to plan.

When time came to select my Dissertation topic, I chose one upon which no other wrote. No, I was not trying to be difficult; I was just Kelly.

Beach Party

◇◇◇◇◇◇◇◇◇◇◇◇◇◇◇◇◇◇◇◇◇

We lived next door to a family who had horses. I frequently hung out with them for the experience. Horses are wonderful beings: powerful, loving animals. I began year-round riding lessons and competed in shows, actually placing. My discipline was Hunter Jumper. I do not recall the exact moment my parents decided, but whenever it was, they settled to buy a horse for me.

My parents and I attended a local auction. Dapple greys, chestnuts, Appaloosas, Quarter Horses, and Thoroughbreds pranced around the ring. Each was gussied up and more than likely buted, reducing any occurance of limping. Bute is an analgesic and anti-inflammatory medication commonly used on horses, which temporarily solves lameness. Dad and I found a beautiful horse upon which he bid. "$1500!" The auctioneer bellowed. Dad rose his hand, and the next thing I knew, Beach Party was ours.

I could not believe my fortune. We did not even have a stall, food, hay, or straw. Details. Details. Right?

My parents sent us to Boarding School, believing that great education would afford us entry into prestigious colleges. Now, before you judge, we had it *good*! Mother and Daddy and even an Aunt and Uncle would come visit. Some classmates' parents dropped them off freshman year and did not see them again until Commencement, two to four years later. Boarding School was tough; don't get me wrong.

My family was reared in the Maryland/District of Columbia area. Mother and Daddy grew up in a segregated world. Their philosophy was if we were educated in other areas, like New England, we stood a better chance of succeeding. Family members participated in social clubs such as Boule, Northeasterners, Links, Alphas, Omegas, Deltas, Jack and Jill, Camping, Soccer, reading, and played musical instruments. When I was five, I told my mother, "Im sick and tired of listening to Bach, Brahms, and Beethoven." She said that's alright, because she bet many of my friends may not know who they were, but I surely did.

To give my experience a trial run, my parents enrolled me into a Boarding School the summer before what would have been my Senior Year in High School Much to their chagrin, I had loads of fun. Mother says I made her a $3,000 flower pot. Truthfully, I do not remember class; however, that was the summer I was introduced to J. D. Salinger's 1951 classic, *Catcher in the Rye*. I also remember, it was the summer Sandra Day O'Connor was appointed to the US Supreme Court and Lady Diana Married Prince Charles.

Had it not been for Boarding School, college would have been a disaster.

Education

◇◇◇◇◇◇◇◇◇◇◇◇◇◇◇◇◇◇◇◇◇◇

I have high expectations. So, I need parents and teachers to encourage me, challenge me to succeed. Prepare me for the future, because it's a changing one. Education is as diverse as the people in the world: history, language, and culture.

Just think about the things we could teach one another. Just think about the activities we could share. So many, the possibilities are endless. Pass the knowledge to me, and when my turn to share comes, I will do the same.

Make me one of your activities and check out my potential.

College

One of my fondest memories, my first year of college, was my father walking me over the bridge; a bridge that later would lead to my sophomore and junior year dorms, and decades later, one over which my husband walked our daughter on a visit to her college just up the road. My Freshwoman year, as we were told to say, as we were NOT men, but women seeking a Liberal Arts Education. I thought I wanted to major in Psycho/Biology. But, my lack of focus and attention, and a little bit of advice from a gentle Biology Professor, "I do not think this is for you," proved to be sound reasons.

Three more attempts at identifying a concentration, I finally declared, a triple major (yah, go figure): English, French, and Third World Relations. Obviously, I was bored.

One week prior to graduation, I was offered a position in Owings Mills, Maryland (MD), working for at Maryland Public Television' Wall $treet Week with Louis Rukeyser. I was the Assistant Director and Producer for the show. This was an exciting job. I kept gold bullion in my house, then a bank safe after my father's urging; visited the Chicago and London Stock Exchanges; was introduced to John W. Rogers Founder & CEO of Aerial Capital Management, who flew to Maryland to take me to lunch; worked with Teddy Ruxpin, and loads of other props for the show.

One evening, we went live because a fly was on the set, buzzing around Louis' head. And in February 1983, 22 inches of snow fell on Maryland, halting traffic everywhere. This caused us to stay late into the night until crews were able to clear roads enough for us to venture home.

But, I suppose one of the greatest secrets, which I found out later, I should have said something, was one Friday, on my way to work, I saw a Mayflower moving van. "Gosh. I wonder who is moving?"

Well, the scoop of the century, and I said nothing. Yep, you got it. The Baltimore Colts, sneaking out on their way to Indianapolis. That's okay. I'm a Skins' fan. Thanks to a relative, we had season tickets. Remember the Hogs?

The Corporation for Public Broadcasting awarded me with Fellowship to work as Producer and Writer at Gallaudet University in Washington, D. C. One requirement for the position was to learn American Sign Language. Every day and night, I practiced so fervently, I signed in my sleep. July 1989, Gallaudet hosted the first Deaf Way Conference, bringing together thousands of deaf and hard of hearing people from around the world. The program on which I worked, F*A*N*T*A*S*T*I*C, was created for deaf and hard of hearing children, and was nominated for an Emmy. My Fellowship soon came to an end. Time to look for something else.

At my cousin's behest, I applied for a job with Xerox Corporation, also in D. C. As a part of my interview, I was challenged to sell a pencil. I earned 212% of my quota. My territory was DuPont Circle!

Xerox held a great deal for me, but I became a little bored. So, I began a Masters Program at Loyola University and part-time work at This End Up Furniture store. Eventually, I added Victoria Secrets to the mix. But, check this out, I married one of my customers from the furniture store. The wedding was full of grandeur, pomp and circumstance, politicians, uniforms, and seating charts, all Christmas time and snow could afford.

Time: It's Ambiguous!

Time is a tool of measurement: 365-days in a year; 24-hours per day. No more; no less. We wish we had more. Why? Hum. Perhaps, people need to plan better. Are you the one who hits the snooze button, only to roll over for another few minutes of shut-eye? Do you move your appointments around the calendar? Do you complain about having too much to do?

Think about what you do on an average day. Create a plan, set some goals. Allow yourself time to get to and from appointments, whatever they may be:

dentist, mani-pedis, school, work, ... Reward yourself when you accomplish a set of necessary goals.

Many complain, "My plate is too full?" Think about if you had nothing to do. You would be bored stiff! You should be grateful when you have something to do. Prioritize. Think. What would you be like be sans activity? Get up. Make a plan. Seize the day.

Who controls your time? One of the things I practiced saying was, "No." I had to make a decision to control my time. I can handle but so much. Prioritize. Be strategic.

Click on to the following link by Lisa Quast, Forbes Contributor.

Happy Planning!

Desert Shield; Desert Storm

Married at the United States Naval Academy, the winter of 1990, when Operation Desert Storm was in full swing, set the scene for a new Military Bride. U. S. Troops were sent to Saudi Arabia by what seemed the thousands. For the first time, Americans experienced live reporting from CNN, which changed war dynamic, as well as for its viewers.

Artists sang ballads with more passion than ever to support our troops. Whitney Houston's *Star Spangled Banner*, Styx's *Show me the way…*, Billy Ray Cyrus *Some gave all…*, Lee Greenwood's *God Bless the U. S. A.*, and the one that always brings a tear, *Voices that Care* written by David Foster, Linda Thompson and Peter Cetera. It was sung by musicians, actors, and athletes. So many people giving of their time and energy. Truly a *Blessed with Activity* venture.

The beeper began to buzz and almost buzzed right off the chair tray. This meant only one thing, Duty calls. An increase in United States (U. S.) Troops and resources had begun. By all means necessary, a coalition of forces were assembled to infiltrate and take down Iraq.

Marj, my Air Force Angel, befriended me during a strange time in my life. War, I had never been through it much less send anyone. When I was in Elementary School, I knew people who had brothers and fathers go fight. But, watching the television, honestly, I did not get the concept for all we were fighting.

Back to Marj. I remember our dinners: every other Tuesday or Thursday. She was a voracious reader, introducing me to a myriad of works and song. We ate our way through Old Town, Virginia but only after one of our manicure appointments.

During the war, I kept myself busy by arriving to work between 6:30 and 7:00 am, leave around 5:00 pm, go to the POAC - Pentagon Officer Athletic Club, go home, shower, change, eat dinner, and return to work. On the weekends, I would drive to either Columbia or Annapolis, MD.

The Toughest Job in the Navy...

◇◇◇

… is the Navy Spouse. Before I was permitted to move to Guam, our Government began shutting down American Bases around the globe. In 1991, just as my Orders were confirmed to leave the East Coast, Naval Base Subic Bay, Philippines, was next to close. Dependent Entries to Guam were halted until further notice. This is when Victoria Secrets came into my life. I also bought a dog, a Red Doberman Pinscher named Zeus. Unbeknownst to me, I would have to crate him, send him ahead of me, via Japan, then to quarantine for four months. Not certain if this was a racket, as Boonie Dogs ran rampant on the island, but I was certain it was. Imagine corrugated tin roofs infested with ticks and fleas. Brewer's yeast and garlic became staples.

On 1 January 1992, I landed in Agana, Guam, tropical island near the Marianas Trench, 30 miles long and eight miles wide. My older cousin concerned a BAP could not live in the middle of the Pacific Ocean. Hum. Well, I needed to find work and keep myself busy and away from the "Grapevine", the infamous rumor mill.

I found work at KUAM/FM/TV shortly after my arrival. An unusual station by all rights. It broadcasted radio as well as television. They would even try to pull programs from the Armed Forces Radio and Television Services.

Weekly, I'd go to the airport to pick up a VHS of *All My Children*. Heavens, though the program was already days behind the States, don't ever let it be missed. Locals would have an attitude if Erica Kane wasn't on their screen each week. I get it. Really. People were extremely friendly. Many thought I was Chamoron.

KUAM was short-lived but really fun. I was soon hired by Sprint International, a major disruptive innovation to many on the island. With the introduction of new services, Sprint offered Islanders an option with cellular service, the perfect competition. MCI had the monopoly on the island. My job was to introduce something new, provide a choice, which made some uncomfortable.

While working for Sprint, I would go home daily to let my dog out. One day, there was a knock at my door. I opened to find a tall, uniformed man, blocking the sun. "Ma'am, there's a bomb in your backyard. You need to evacuate the premises". He was rather insistent.

"But what about my dog? I asked.
Sergeant's response, "I don't care, but you must go!"Me, I've gotta continue the conversation. "How'd it get there? Where is it?"

"Ma'am, some workers were digging a trench. One of their tools hit the object and called it in. Now, Ma'am, I really need you to go!"

Boy was this going to be something exciting in the next Newsletter to the family back in the States. Mother will be thrilled. Not!

Frustration

◇◇◇◇◇◇◇◇◇◇◇◇◇◇◇◇◇◇◇◇

Living with someone who is always frustrated can be challenging. You have a choice. You can agree and fall in line, or you can move on with your activities not letting any negativity affect you.

Remember. Misery loves company. And, you are judged by the company you keep. This company has names: depression, heartbreak, sadness, dejection ...many others can participate as well. Up to you if you want to let them in.

So, what are your options? Frustration stems from how we believe others should behave, how things should work, and how we believe people should treat us. Our expectations are great. Well, you can't always have what you want. Hold on to your "beliefs, perspectives, likes, ideals, and values" but be willing to learn something new and possibly uncomfortable (Vilhauer, 2015, para. 1).

Don't let the activity of others frustrate you. Often, your actions and the actions of others may turn to aggression. If this is the case, seek help. I am by no means a professional, but I have seen signs in many people, including myself. Yuk! Frustration is sadness masked, permitting others to see the chink in our armor, an area of vulnerability. Think about performing a SWOT Analysis on yourself: Strengths, Weaknesses, Opportunities, and Threats. Pick three each for each letter and work on them for you.

Consider yourself first.

Sandeman

◇◇◇◇◇◇◇◇◇◇◇◇◇◇◇◇◇◇

Shortly after our arrival to Rota, Spain, two weeks, I'm certain, I was in the kitchen preparing dinner. Mind you, we were at the Navy Lodge. Not much room, yet wide enough to spread my arms. The kids were six and 18 months. Slicing an avocado for salad was the intention. Well, that never occured. Next thing I know, the walls resemble a scene in Chainsaw Massacre! Trying to manage the situation, my little one walks in, "Mommy, what's happening?"

I couldn't panic her. I'm not even certain I felt pain. "Nothing", I replied. "I need to go outside."

I scoured and searched for anyone who could help. I called out to Housing Keeping staff who came running. The manager took me to the ER, and some kind staffer watched the children. Without getting too graphic, I went into surgery to have nerves and tendons reattached. Great going for a Senior Spouse just arriving at the Command. Oh, well. I'm human, right?

Grateful for the location, we toured France, Portugal, Gibraltar, and North Africa. I was even medevaced to Landstuhl Regional Medical Center, Germany, because of a nodule on my larynx. Mother flew from Maryland to care for the children in my absence. Such a beautiful, intelligent woman. She'd drop everything for her family.

Nodules form because of acute trauma or chronic irritation. My voice would vasolate between Lauren Bacall and Minnie Mouse. Raspy and hoarse, I made an appointment with the Otorhinolaryngologist. She discovered the nodules and said I have two options: fly back to Bethesda or Germany. Not knowing what my medical condition was, I said Germany. I've been to D. C. I have family there!

So, off I went. Spent a week in Landstuhl, Germany, relearning how to speak, learning not to whisper. Did you know that is bad for your vocal chords? At any rate, my treatment went rather well. When I flew home, one of the Corpsman noticed I had Asthma. Nonchalantly responding to her, saying yes, things began to happen. My trip over was uneventful, landing in Italy three times then to Germany. My condition was elevated to Asthmatic. I was placed in a seat with an Oxygen tank and monitored all the way home.

I do not like to draw attention to my illness or my allergy. People panic, making the situation worse. For some reason, medical staff thought it prudent to pre-board and monitor me monitor me closely. I am grateful.

My role as a Senior Military Spouse varied. But, the most important role was making certain my children led a "normal" life. I wanted my children to play with other children: officer, enlisted, civilian. After all, I wasn't wearing the stripes or stars. Important to me was rearing children who were happy, healthy, and spiritually sound. Let 'em play in the dirt. Let 'em roll around. Let 'em run naked in the sprinkler. One Halloween, the kids dressed up as Marie from

Disney's Aristocats and Winnie the Pooh's Tigger. Only problem was when my son put on his costume, Tigger didn't bounce. :-(

Thoughts+Words+Actions=What will come to you

Your thoughts are free. They belong to you. What you do with them is your business. However, be prepared to understand them, for what you think and what you do is who you become. Is your glass half full or empty?

Ponder your thoughts for a moment. Are you a person who blames and makes excuses, therefore becoming a victim? Or are you an authentic person, realizing accountability for your thoughts, words, and actions? What you see and what others see (in you) can be an awareness builder. A reality check.

Sometimes your opinion will matter, sometimes. Are you familiar with your character? The capacity of your thoughts and actions are measured by responses. Perhaps, this is an exercise in understanding. "We must admit the vanity of our false distinctions" (Kennedy, n. d., para 1). The tricky part is, are you mindful of recognizing "qualities ... you [may not] consciously acknowledge" (McKenzie, n. d., para. 2)? Say that 10 times fast!

Except everything as it is. Somethings can be changed. You have to be willing to accept if you are part of the problem or the solution.

26

◇◇◇◇◇

Then, I received *the* call. "Everyone is alright." It was 3:00 am, and I sat straight up in bed not really comprehending what I just heard. "Everyone escaped with minor injuries."

"Wait! What happened," I asked.
"Our plane crash veered off the runway. The left wing clipped a bunker [in Souda Bay, Crete] on landing".

Unfortunately, a young female pilot went long on the runway, and the plane crashed into the ground. This was the second time I received a report about a female pilot. The first was in 1994, when Kara Hultgreen crashed on final approach into the USS Abraham Lincoln. I know this because the case was reviewed in my home.

At any rate, my job was to speak with the Chaplain, the spouses, and work with the Ombudsman. The biggest problem, at the moment, was getting the equipment and plane out of Greece. The EP-3 Orion is furnished with anti-submarine and maritime surveillance equipment. As the investigation mounted, I was permitted to see the official and unofficial photographs of the plane. Life stood in the balance, as we did not know if that was a career ending event. So, we held our breath, prayed, and did what we could to keep life on point.

The Admiral once told me, "You are more powerful than you think." In hindsight, I suppose, wish I knew that then. We were attending an event in Rota, Spain, shortly after the Squadron's Navy EP-3 Orion, an anti-submarine plane, crashed in Greece. We were heading for Admiral but never got there.

Children DO learn what they live

In such a large world, each of us has much to learn and even teach. Teaching begins at home. Whether this is a good place or bad. Then, we take these lessons to the streets and emulate what has been taught. Only by imitation and affirmation do we continue to pass these lessons along.

Children do not realize differences until they near five years of age. Then, the questions come. I remember when my children asked about the Rainbow Flag. "Why so many colors?" they asked. I told them, the colors represented variety, diversity of people. They accepted my answer sans any doubt. Only when they became the only brown children in class, did they ask about color and differences in people. Unfairly, they were treated differently, because that's what other families and cultures "imprinted" on their classmates.

I, as others, would like to propose peace and understanding. Have your neighbor educate you about his or her culture. Only when we begin to understand one another will we establish relationships. Do not hate someone for the color of his or her skin. Instead, ask, "Tell me about yourself."

War College

◇◇◇◇◇◇◇◇◇◇◇◇◇◇◇◇◇◇◇◇◇◇

"Never interrupt your enemy when he is making a mistake." ~ Sun Tzu

In 1998, we moved to Fort Adams State Park, well, just the outskirts where Military Housing was situated. Great water views, walks, bike riding, and wonderful playgrounds for the kids. Oh, and during the winter, snow fell so great, the BIG hill was an experience. The first time the kids went sledding.

Fort Adams was also a place where so many families lived. Many of the kids ended up at our house, for parents would say, "Go to Miss Kelly's House. She's always got something going." Truth be told, I did. I had two boxes of costumes out of which neighborhood children would pick their characters. We'd make cookies, plant seeds, make snowmen and women! Create a batch of playdough and play board games. I never minded, after all, the kids were in my zone. I knew who they were, as well as their parents.

You have a Choice

◇◇◇◇◇◇◇◇◇◇◇◇◇◇◇◇◇◇◇◇◇◇◇◇◇◇◇◇◇◇◇◇◇◇◇◇

My girlfriend and I were talking about the blog. Next thing you know, I get this text. I asked her before I use it, what would be her spin on the above saying. 'Cause would have said, we have so many things that could keep us occupied and so many distractions, sometimes ya' gotta just let things go. Be grateful for what you have. Well, she showed me a different thought.

"I wrote a love letter to David Cassidy when I was seven years old. I walked to the mailbox and tried to buy a stamp from the mail carrier himself so I didn't have to borrow one from my parents so they didn't know I was writing the letter. Of course, I couldn't buy one. I got up the courage to go to my dad and ask to borrow a stamp. His question of course was why? I had to bare my soul. He simply said let me teach you an important lesson .... never write anything down. That's the quickest way for people to find out everything. Maybe he was burned in young love once..."

"As an adult, writing is the most relaxing and therapeutic form of relief. Whether it be diet notes, letters to an old friend, writing thoughts down in prep for a dreaded discussion or encounter; it works!"

"Dad gave me the stamp. David never responded."

Thanks, LB ~ef

California Here We Come

◇◇

In 1999, we drove cross country to our new Duty Station, San Diego, CA, where I *just knew* we would only be there for two years. As we crossed the California border, we sang I Love Lucy's *California here we come!* Well, 18 years later; I'm still here. My daughter recently earned her Master of Science in Education; my son will walk next May with a Bachelors in Black Studies and pursue Law.

In 2000, many things changed. My now Ex, returned from a six-month WestPAC deployment, and I called quits. After 10 years of silence, I could take no more. If you've ever read Anita Shreve's *Pilot's Wife*, you may understand. What goes on det, stays on det.

In 2003, I married a San Diego Native Boy who professes, "We need a native lane!" We've had our challenges but love one another like crazy. He was willing to give up his home, because the children and I had to move out of our rental in Bonita, CA.

Throughout the years, as a new family, we did Daddy Daughter Dances, Mother Son dates, Scouts, Soccer, Football my Masters and Doctorate, YMCA sleepovers, Octoparty, …

My, how time flies

◇◇◇◇◇◇◇◇◇◇◇◇◇◇◇◇◇◇◇◇◇◇◇◇◇◇◇◇◇◇◇◇◇◇◇◇◇◇

Many of us say, we do not have enough time _____. You fill in the blank. Many reasons exist because of those feelings. Consider the following, and mind you, I am not a Mathematician.

Twenty-four hours in a day, seven days in a week, and 365 days in a year. That is unless it's Leap Year in which are 366. Therefore, we have 8,760 hours in a year (Leap Year = 8, 784). The average work year, for the full-time employee, is 2,080 hours. This leaves 6,680 hours to pretty much choose what we want. So, what is the problem?

According to Jayson DeMeyers (2015), Founder of AudienceBloom, seven scientific explanations exist why people mutter, "'there aren't enough hours in the day

'" (para. 1), espousing if they only had more time, missions could be accomplished. The world, as a matter of generality, operates on a 9-5 clock. But how people use time is a factor in their daily lives.

DeMeyers (2015) says, there are scientific reasons people say they do not have time:

1. You Don't Wake Up Early.

2. You multitask.

3. You Don't Practice Time Management.

4. You aren't getting enough rest.

5. You're too concerned with time.

6. You're pessimistic.

7. You're Too Engrossed in Your Work. (para. 2-8)

We can't control time, But, what we can do is rearrange our habits. Remember the 21-day test? Reframe your thoughts and actions. Take the 21-day challenge. Also, consider, you are Blessed with Activity. Now, prioritize.

Ziggy

◇◇◇◇◇◇◇◇◇

Always busy; always running. My husband says he has a spastic quadruped (Wire Haired Fox Terrier, Ziggy) and a biped – that'd be me. I neglected to tell him about these dogs. To get from one side of the room, they may traverse the furniture.

In 2005, I had this urge to get a puppy. I stalked the Internet looking for just the right one. Then I found him. With a spot on his hind quarter and a spark in his eye, I said, "He's the one!" Pick of the litter, of course, I communicated with the breeder for weeks, wondering just how I would get this pup from Hawaii to California. That's right, Hawaii! Unbeknownst to me, my husband contacted the breeder and made a deal. Later, she calls me to tell me the pup had been sold. I hung up the phone to say the search ended, as Ziggy had a new home.

"That's because I bought him. He's yours." As tears flowed from his face, the two of us embraced almost hysterically, as I realized, Ziggy's new home was here.

"So, Mom, don't just stand there; let us in!"

Dogs; they are our partners, family members, assistants, support, ...
They watch over us, play with us, and often remind us to keep moving. Our
middle pup, yes, she was about 11 months in that picture, is preparing us for
grandchildren. We put all of her toys in a basket by the door. Only for her to
pull each of them out, scattering them around the house. Hum!

Playing with our dogs actually minimizes our stress, increasing our hormones: serotonin and dopamine, which help reduce stress levels and help improve memory and concentration. Somedays, admittedly, things become a little chaotic with a 14 yro, 6 yro, and an almost 2 yro. But, we wouldn't have it any other way. When I come home from work, a cacophony of barks welcomes me, as I walk thru the front door. Doesn't get any better than this.

Organized Chaos?

◇◇◇◇◇◇◇◇◇◇◇◇◇◇◇◇◇◇◇◇◇◇◇◇◇◇◇◇◇◇◇◇◇◇

"In the midst of chaos, there is opportunity."

I remember a commercial where the woman could bring home the bacon and fry it up in a pan. God gave women hips to carry babies and groceries and brains to run the first business, the house.

Now a day, both men and women take on the management role of the home. Thanks to Women's Liberation, men and women are in the workplace, as well as home. A blessing, at times, to juggle family, work, and life. Necessary in today's world to keep food on the table, bills paid, and children (and adults) busy.

Living an active life is a choice. Balancing it takes patience and skill. If you become despondent about it, you have a choice to change it. Look at your calendar. Plan your tasks. Give yourself buffer zones: time to get to and from an event. Put time in for you. The other option is to be bored stiff! Then what?

Do not complain about the amount of activity you have. Work smart, not hard.

Use a scheduling system, create an outline. You can always fill your plate. Consider the things you must do versus the things you want to do. Prioritize. No need to complain. If you were not blessed with activity, where would you be?

The reason I have a Suburban!

Many reasons I have a Suburban. First is safety. Second, I can haul practically anything, including the 72 pizzas my daughter asked me to pick up for ASB, "Don't worry Mom. They're already paid for!" I could carry the kids and their friends, which included soccer and football players. Note to self, "Always roll down the windows, all of them!"

My Suburbans, yes, I've had three, are great for airport runs, grocery shopping, and just for me driving around town or on work trips up the coast.

I've driven a Suburban since I was 16. Even took one to college. Road trip! A few times, the women in my dorm would take rides to church, West Point, New York, and home on the holidays. Back then, I only charged about $15 for the ride south, as gas was about $1.30/gallon. Imagine what I could get now!

Simple Abundance

About 15 years ago, my husband gifted me with one ton of dirt! That $73 Mother's Day gift has given me so much pleasure. I am one with my soil.

Other than spending time with my family, I love working with my plants. Most of which we can eat. No pesticides, no questionable preservatives, nothing funny in the soil. Planting roses and tomatoes was my only goal. Twelve avocado trees later, I'm a mini-farmer. I'm proud. I share my bounty with friends and neighbors, giving each piece away freely. Sometimes, neither the fruit nor vegetables get to the house. They become treats, as I make my way through the yard. Hum. Yummy.

I grow herbs (parsley, basil, oregano, rosemary, and cilantro), mint (chocolate, spearmint, peppermint, apple, mint mint, and sweet mint), tomatoes (Mr. Stripey, Roma, Big Girl, and yellow), Grapefruit, orange, lime, and an Asian citrus psyllid tree, which cross bred with my other citrus trees. Gracious! Last, a pink guava, pomegranate, cucumbers, and squash.

I've duplicated one of my favorite nursery's environment complete with water fountains and wind chimes, creating my Place of Zen. As I check each plant, I walk ever so carefully not to step into the dogs' recent gifts.

My Garden

◇◇◇◇◇◇◇◇◇◇◇◇◇◇◇◇◇◇◇◇◇◇◇◇◇◇

I've always loved gardening. Perhaps, the bug bit me when visiting Mr. & Mrs. Leslie Gray from Plymouth, Massachusetts. They were friends of my paternal grandparents. The thought of growing food took me by storm. Years later, I put my daughter in a Kelty and began gardening in Virginia. In a tiny backyard garden, I grew tomatoes, jalapenos, and eggplants. When we arrived in Rota, Spain, I grew Anaheim Peppers, tomatoes, and bougainvillea.

Gardens are a blessing, which bring food, wealth, and peace into the home.

Wealth. Just what is it?

I honestly had a difficult time with this one, trying to choose the "right" image to express wealth. So, I went straight to my garden. That is, short of showing photos of my family (the most important, valuable entity, thing, item, gift in the world to me), my garden has provided a wealth of nourishment.

Ever consider just what wealth really is? It's not just one dimensional, believing affluence, prosperity, an abundance of resources, substance, fortune are it. What about your loved ones? Your health? Your spirituality? Your happiness? I am the richest woman in the world because of my family and friends.

"Stop and smell the roses" may be a cliché (Kennelly, 2012, para. 1); however, it conjures meanings from satisfaction to appreciation for things in our lives. The aroma of a rose brings happiness to the senses. Acknowledging the richness in something, as simple as a rose, creates an emotional connection. Consider what Nature has done to create this woody, prickly plant. Now, ponder those in your life.

Finding appreciation and gratitude for your family and friends, health, job - even volunteering, are sources of goodness and wealth. Next time you think about someone who lives in a particular neighborhood or drives a certain car, ask yourself, is he or she as wealthy as I am?

It's just stuff, right?

◇◇

I think I'm at the stage where stuff is just stuff. A term I learned, as a military spouse, was "Dustable". You know, those little chotskies, nicknacks that just hang out on your shelves collecting dust. My aunt and grandmother began giving away things as they aged. Wondering why, I asked, "How come"? Their response often was, "Because I can't take it with me and want you to have it." By giving things away while they were living meant less for people to clear afterwards, too.

Well, I'm at that stage. Not planning to go anywhere, soon, I would rather give things away, knowing the gesture might make someone smile: relative, friend, or through community donation. The point is, I've been blessed with ever so much. I would be remiss if I did not share. Anthony J. D'Angelo said it best, "The most important things in life aren't things".

Possessions are just that, something controlled or owned. What about possessing good health. Your health is your wealth. It is a gift to nurture, not a possession to protect. Josef Pieper says, "'Everything gained and everything claimed follows upon something given, and comes after something gratuitous and unearned; that in the beginning there is always a gift'" (Jenkins, 2016, para. 8). Think carefully who and what are essential in your life.

Consider your stuff. Let it go. After all, it's just stuff.

Your time to do the dishes

My siblings and I had chores - four of us, more than enough to go around. Mother crafted a chart numbered 1-4, which she placed on the inside of the kitchen cabinet, an easy location for us to find when we were curious, as to what day and chore we had. Needless to say, we would avoid that door at all costs.

"Your turn to do the dishes", calls Mother. Would you believe I challenged her? She wasn't too certain who was going to make through puberty first, her or me!

Early Saturday Mornings, Daddy would march us downstairs, as we grumbled, guiding us to the unpleasant task of clearing out the garage, cleaning the attic (that was always in July!), weeding out to the Rock Garden (imagine my little sister waiving dandelions like Ferdinand the Bull), or mowing the lawn, further noting, chores stood between us and fun.

Chores, we were told, kept the house and property clean. It was a matter of pride, taking care of our home, a tradition. We learned responsibility and just how hard and long we could work. Cleaning became family recreation, which we never saw at the time. Unbeknownst to us, those activities brought us together.

In recent generations, chores have fallen out of favor. People become resentful even emotional when asked to pick up, wash, or sweep something. Obviously, the choice is yours. I've learned the argument was not worth it. Mother was extremely strong, dealing with prepubescent teenagers griping to clean. Perhaps, if I hadn't fussed, I would know what the vacuum cleaner bag was.

Thanks, Mother and Daddy.

Quilting

◇◇◇◇◇◇◇◇◇◇◇◇◇◇

I began quilting to keep me busy. Then, I found it was truly an art in which I could participate. My mother and grandmother could sew like there was no tomorrow. Mother could create. For one High School event, masterfully and magically made a two-piece suit for me in one evening, like the Shoemaker and his Elves. The green suit appeared on my door the morning of my event. It had pockets, pleats, yoke, darts, seams, … Me? I sew straight lines. I tried sewing halters and knitting sweaters. You are better off purchasing them in a store! As you can tell, Ziggy thinks the quilt is a new rug for him.

The Zoo Lady

Every child should have a pet. Well, that is how I was raised. We even snuck a few in to the house. Eventually, I would tell Mother - waited to tell Dad until the pet (gerbil, hamster, rabbit, fish) had been home for a while.

I brought home a fat hamster one day. Thought I was good to go. Half the time, I didn't tell my folks I brought in a new pet. Well, I got her to my room - so pleased with myself. Well, three days later, she delivered 12 babies! Yikes! A couple of weeks into the new family, one of the babies got lose. Shimmied up and out of the cage, ran down the hall (without the dogs noticing), and climbed up my parents' bedroom drapes! Next thing I heard was my father calling, "Kelly! Come in here." Can't be good. Right? The baby was squeaking so loudly at Dad, as he tried to get him from top of the rail.

Another time, I brought home a rabbit named Shalimar. One day, he got lose. The only way I found out was my mother heard a lot of rustling upstairs. Come to find, our Wire Haired Fox Terrier pinned Shalimar into a corner. Thank goodness for the spaces in the wicker chair. All the dog could do was lick him.

Because of the wonderful time having pets, I thought my kids should experience the same. A times, however, I think we went a little too far: two dogs, two Russian Tortoise, a Hermit Crab, a Cichlid, and two Guinea Pigs - who later had babies!

And then, there were three! The unconditional love we give each other is amazing. Though the up and down, back and forth to door can be maddening, we would not be without them.

To Do List

<><><><><><><><><><><><><><><><><>

Ya wanna talk "Blessed with Activity?" Well, here it is! If you do not have a dog, you may not understand this, and if you do, you may be rolling over laughing your a** off!

The first time my husband and I saw this sign, we knew we had to have it. It truly depicts our life.

Once upon a time, we put a bell on the door, training our dog to let us know when he wanted to go out. Successful. He pawed the bell; we came a runnin'. We'd let him out, let him in, we'd sit, he'd ring the bell, we'd come runnin'. Get the picture? Needless to say, the bell was removed. He was training us!

See Obstacles as Opportunities

◇◇

What we often see as obstacles are really opportunities for us to spread our wings to challenge fate. Often, we think the grass is greener on the other side. Is it really? B. C. Forbes said, *"History has demonstrated that the most notable winners usually encountered heart-breaking obstacles before they triumphed. They won because they refused to become discouraged by their defeats"* (n. d.).

So, consider these few things to increase activity toward yourself. Set a goal and follow the recipe below:

1. Remove drama from your life.

2. Ask for assistance, directions to the "Yellow Brick Road".

3. Seek vital resources before you make crucial decisions.

4. Consider the obstacle in front of you. Assess it; evaluate it. Work to move it. In other words, get the tools to get rid of it!

5. Stay focused now. This is the point the opportunity to move that obstacle could be a challenge.

6. Be disciplined. Be good to yourself. Challenges can make us stronger. Chip away at this obstacle, one piece at a time.

7. Repeat steps as necessary.

Celebrate your success!

We swim through troubled waters

✕✕✕

because our enemies can't

✕✕✕

Though this is not the exact quote (thank you LM for sharing), I've done some research only to find the saying in a few places sans an author.

Each of us face challenges at one time or another and with varied extremes. Rising thru the pain, you are not alone. Others may be going through something similar. This is a time to focus your attention on them, sharing your storm.

Make peace with your past, so it does not destroy your present. You run the risk of letting it shape you. The past can consume you, swallow your energy, take possession of your spirit. Come to terms with pain, anger, and sadness, as your health will be affected.

See someone. Make a call. Be honest with yourself. That's the first step.

Stay Busy to Avoid Sadness

"Active natures are rarely melancholy. Activity and sadness are incompatible."

– *Christian Bovee*

We were speaking with my mother-n-law a couple of days ago. She called crying after I sent her a Bitmoji, wishing her Happy Mother's Day. "No one has ever said that to me before. Thank you. You all are so good to me," she said.

A widow, now for two years, my mother-n-law has begun to do things she's not done for 30 years: swim and hit a golf ball. Rather than wallow in her sorrow, she gets up and moves. Seventy-four, working at Home Depot full-time, no grass grows under her feet.

So, for anyone reading this, let me first say, I am not a Psychologist. But, I do know what will chase sorrow:

1. Make a new friend

2. Join a club

3. Volunteer

4. Garden, even if it is in your kitchen window. Watch what you planted grow!

The great thing about having a garden is the exchange of carbon dioxide and oxygen between you and the plant. According to Rebecca Straus (2017), "A recently published analysis of scientific studies on how gardening impacts health has some fascinating insights into how digging in the dirt benefits your mind, body, and soul—not just your soil".

5. Find a hobby

6. Go to school

The point here is the list of things to do is endless. Get out of your way. Remember the Abominable Snowman in Rudolph the Red-nosed-Reindeer? Well, he had to put one foot in front of the other, ...

Coexisting

◇◇◇◇◇◇◇◇◇◇◇◇◇◇◇

"Can't we all just get along" (Brownson, 2016, para. 1)? King's quote paraphrased.

In the midst of wars and discontent, those of us who remain home should take time to understand one another, learn about one another, ... while men and women are fighting for our freedom. Enough said here, as I do not want to engage in religious or political conversation.

BUT, if we could see each other for our differences, wouldn't it be cool if we could share in them? Think about food festivals: different flavors and textures melded together to make something scrumptious. Many years ago, my father took me on a mini-road trip through Lancaster, Pennsylvania. We stopped to eat at Good 'N Plenty, a restaurant, know well for its Family Style Dinners. I thought, "Oh heavens! Why am I breaking bread with strangers?" But that was the point! Break bread with a stranger and learn something about him or her. Thanks, Dad.

Think about spaghetti. Its etymology traces back to "Talmud in the 5th century AD" (Julia, 2011, para. 1). Think about the egg roll, omelette, or the Gyeran-mari. You know that rolled thing stuffed with cabbage, vegetables, and meat? The point is, we share so many things: language, food, traditions, yet, we neglect to give credit where credit is due. So, why not open up a conversation? Get busy, create an activity and get to know your neighbor.

Communication

Hashtag this. Hashtag that. Ever get confused? Feel left behind? Whatever happened to full sentences? LMAO. ILY. GTG. BFF. AMA. AFAIK. OMG. SMH. Get the picture?

A friend of mine and I were texting, this morning. I knew better, as I was still under the covers and not fully awake. But, I was giving it the ol' college try. She typed something. I responded. She typed something else. Didn't take long before we were confused about what the other wrote. I looked for an Emoji to express my frustration. Ever feel that way?

Once, I dictated a message to Siri for my husband. You know where this is going, right? Well, I just knew "she" received everything I said and in the correct order. Well, the sweet, lovely message delivered to him was, "You need to get an attorney!". OMG! Are you kidding?!? Thank goodness, he does not rely on texting, as much as many of us. I got to him before he opened his messages.

And, then, there is autocorrect! Ever feel as though your conversation is lost in translation? One conversation I saw said, "I have my key, so lick foot if you want too". The sentence was supposed to say, "I have my keys, so lock door if you want too".

My kids have become rather patient with me. Then again, I can hear them shouting, "Mom! Just type! STOP using Siri. You are not making sense!" Gosh, then why do I have the darn thing? I mean, it's not like I'm asking her to pour me coffee. Though, that would be nice.

My point is modern advancements have affected our means of communication and how we relate to others. Social media plays such a prominent role in our lives, we forget how to correspond, relate, associate with one another. Perhaps, we should take a timeout every once in a while and articulate, converse with our voices, ... hey face-to-face. Hum.

Can't It Wait?

◇◇◇◇◇◇◇◇◇◇◇◇◇◇◇◇◇◇◇◇◇◇◇◇◇◇◇◇◇◇◇◇◇◇◇◇◇

I remember when cell phones first came out. They were literally as big as bricks. If you had one, you thought your stuff did not stink. Furthermore, the brick had only numbers. As phones got smaller, technology got better, sending messages via our phones was fascinating. We could get twice as much done in just a short amount of time. Text me the grocery list, text me the directions, text me your picture, text me..... Then, we took texting to the next level.

Have you ever seen people shaving while driving? Putting on makeup while driving, reading the newspaper ... while driving? Really? Well, now there's

<u>typing while driving</u>. I can nearly get my lipstick on much less hold my cup of coffee. And, if you drive a stick, *forget about it*! So, truth-be-told, I've texted and stopped.

I want to come home to my family at night. I want to meet friends for coffee, exercise, and read. If you or I feel bigger and badder than the rest, we are hypocrites. Driving is a blessed activity and grand responsibility, a privilege not a right, which must be taken seriously.

<u>Pass this on</u>. Perhaps, someone will listen to you. Perhaps, someone will listen to me. Perhaps, someone will listen to them.

Knowledge is Power

◇◇◇◇◇◇◇◇◇◇◇◇◇◇◇◇◇◇◇◇◇◇◇◇◇◇◇◇◇

A most recognizable Proverb, *Knowledge is Power* means one has the ability sans physical strength to use his or her brain to interpret impulses, which are sent by neurons, creating messages. These messages may define smell, taste, touch, ... You categorize them and use them where need be.

Wanting to find ways to keep my brain engaged and intact, I read *Daring to Live Fully*, and wanted to share. Since this is Commencement Season, time couldn't be more perfect.

Your brain is full of energy and to keep it going, you must fuel your body: back bone connected to the neck bone connected to the head bone type thing. Minimize stress; eat/drink antioxidants: green tea, blueberries, and chocolate (the darker the better); sleep (though some believe it is overrated and do not need much), eat Omega-3s and Turmeric, exercise, and have sex! Yes, I said Sex.

Enhancing cognitive functions will help the brain develop. Learning never stops. Exercise your brain and see what happens.

Reading

◇◇◇◇◇◇◇◇◇◇◇◇◇◇◇◇

Reading leads to the awareness of the world around us. It enhances our ability to travel, converse, and live.

Reading is a means of communication, a privilege once denied to many. Some readings, I used to feel were rather daunting, like do I really have to read this? The problem is reading is a barrier between the have and the have nots, which stemmed from slavery, when White owners did not want slaves reading about freedom in the North.

Segregated and low-income schools could not always afford proper resources to educate and care for students. Often, textbooks were used, out of date, and no longer relevant. Mark Keierkeber (2018) reflects, "education funding disparities often leave schools ill-equipped to provide students an adequate education" (para. 1).

Even today, the Academic Performance Index for Public Schools in low-income, minority areas suffer. The disproportioned "funding inequities leave cash-strapped schools without adequate access to effective teachers and technology [further falling] short on the most basic classroom supplies like textbooks, desks — and even toilet paper" (Keierkeber, 2018, para. 2). How are our children and even adults supposed to get along if the basic needs are not met?

My focus has changed a bit, as I have been reading some pretty heavy books. Read them before your judge: *The Shack, The Walk, White Trash: The 400-Year Untold History of Class in America, I Know Why the Caged Bird Sings, and Twelve Years a Slave* .

My point is literacy is freedom. When you read or have someone read to you, you are transported to a place, gleaning knowledge of another land, power, people, even entertainment, ... True power. Give the gift of reading.

Matthew Gartland (2012) asks his readers to describe in three words, what reading was to them.

- Douglas Donegani – A world inside me.
- Graeme McNee – The human experience.
- Jackie – Escape from reality.
- The Literary Analyst – Art illuminating truth.
- Mindy Holahan – An emotional touchstone.
- Mitch Allen – Time well spent.
- Mom2hannahs – A soul exposed.
- Nick Thacker – A change catalyst.
- Paul Jun – Life making sense.
- Ritu Rao – Pleasure without guilt.
- Toni – A secret handshake. (para. 2)

So, I leave you with this. Give a book or a giftcard - gotta remember technology. Take someone to the library and give him or her a library card. You've just given the give of knowledge. Now, see what happens.

Mindfulness

<><><><><><><><><><><><><><><><><><><><><>

Are you present in your daily activities? Or are you mentally someplace else? Tending to yourself should be priority: feelings, thoughts, and bodily sensations. As you would schedule a doctor's appointment or grocery shop, block space for yourself into the calendar. Trivia or propaganda may dwell in your mind. Take control. Identify a means by which to practice mindfulness.

Mindfulness can be accomplished through exercise, mediation, and by the way, it's free. You already have mindfulness within you. You just need to learn how to bring it forth and experience it.

Methods of obtaining mindfulness can be found around the Internet. Personally, I like to workout, listen to books, work in my garden - well, it's not really work. Often, when my husband looks for me, he finds me in the garden, talking with my plants. You ever play in the dirt?

Playing in the dirt actually elevates your mood; some say it may actually lift depression, which can help stimulate your immune system. Think about kids on the playground. Aren't they in a much better mood after burning off energy and swallowing dirt?

Wear Your China

◇◇

How many of you have Grandmother's China? Or, for that matter, have China you were given for a wedding gift? Do you use it? Or, is it in a box packed away in storage?

Looking at the picture above, I am not saying you should repurpose your grandmother's china, but what the heck are you doing with it? I have china and crystal from my wedding; my husband has his mother's. Wait, I believe I even have my maternal grandmother's, and some of my parents' silver - the real stuff in velvet, a bit oxidized, too. Why not use it?

Pulling "the good stuff" out for special occasions is marvelous. Why not use it more often? Anyone have the red "You are special, today" plate?

China was created to be used, not to be stored, or collect dust. These treasured items should be used throughout the week! Create an excuse for a celebration. Don't wait for a fancy day. Put some tofu or hamburger on those plates! If they chip or scratch, replace them or wear them. Hang them on the wall if you do not want anyone to touch them. But for heaven's sake, get them out of those boxes!

Point is, sometimes we tend to stray from the simple pleasures in life. Consider treating yourself to a new tradition. Enjoy things you have or get rid of them!

My husband and I were walking the neighborhood and came upon an Estate Sale. Wouldn't you know it, the woman who lived in the house had four full sets of china. We purchased one set for $200. Now, what am I going to do with it? At the time, we thought it a good idea. We were saving them - from what we did not know. Preserving them for history. Now, that set too, sits in a box in our attic. Time to break it out, position it, wear it, or donate it.

Follow Your Dreams

◇◇◇◇◇◇◇◇◇◇◇◇◇◇◇◇◇◇◇◇◇◇◇◇◇◇◇◇◇◇◇◇◇

Richard Bach, author of *Jonathan Livingston Seagull* (1970), tells the story of a seagull simply bored with daily routine. Jonathan discovered a passion to fly, hoping to liberate himself from the day's norm. Based upon and dedicated to Jonathan Livingston, a second-generation aviator after the Wright Brothers, Livingston and Jonathan, committed themselves to learn everything they could about soaring about the earth into the clouds. They began a trek to follow their dreams.

Jonathan Living Seagull was unwilling to compromise what he believed. Through dedicated tenacity, he learned to be at peace with whom he was, as long as he was able to lead a happy life.

Bach's words have been with me since the first day I read his book. Not truly understanding the full meaning of the book until later did I come to respect Jonathan. So, whenever I see a seagull, though I may chase him or her away from my food, I shall always respect the figure, as it holds something true and strong in spirit.

I've had many dreams. Each may not be precisely organized or well-defined, but they are goals, keeping me focused and positive no matter what barriers I may face.

Watching Your Children Grow!

◇◇

A hard lesson for me to realize is I was the "vessel" who carried my children for 38 weeks. I delivered them to the world, cared for them until they could care for themselves, loved them, guided them, supported them, and now, I must step aside and watch. That, right there, became difficult for me to swallow (yes, there goes the umbilical cord snapping!); they are a part of the world, making lives for themselves.

If you are lucky, you will spend 18 summers with your child(ren) and blessed if they have ten fingers and toes. My babies kept me going. Never bored, we were active: went on adventures, travelled, sang songs, created an art studio in the garage, played sports, pumpkin patched, watched movies, ate pizza and popcorn on Friday nights.

At an early age, we began to fly, surprising passengers just how quiet the children were. One trip, we crossed the Atlantic Ocean from Rota, Spain to Delaware. Boarding the C-130, I carried two carseats, luggage, oh yes, one toddler, and an infant. Some felt sorry for me. I think; or maybe I was just so slow ascending the stairs, a few decided to assist. After each flight, strangers walked up to us, saying thank you. Shaking my head, I didn't understand. "Your children are so quiet, we never knew they were even on the plane."

Thanks to my children, life became extraordinary and gave me a greater purpose to live.

Hanging out with my adult children is visiting the best parts of the village who raised them. The village, a community of people, interacted with them, teaching life's lessons: good and bad. Through those lessons, they helped these young adults experience and evolve in a safe environment, to prioritize, to learn from mistakes, to cherish relationships, to share, and to love.

Those children are no longer "mine". I just brought them into the world. Now, it's theirs.

Just look for me; I'll be
◇◇◇
on the 50 yard line!
◇◇◇

Attending my kids' Soccer and Football games was ever important to me. When they looked up into the stands, I wanted them to know I was there, rooting them on, … well, screaming! Yes, I was the loud parent. Team Parents knew, "The 50-yard line is Kelly's". I also wanted my kids to know about the sacrifices made for them. Tuition for primary and secondary schools can be rather expensive and dip into your retirement funds.

The other thing my children saw was the top of my head, literally. I was working on my Doctorate. So, at each opportunity I had, I would bring a book or something to read. I'd advise completing your schooling pre-kids, but I would not have traded that experience for the world.

I now have my Doctorate in Health Administration; my daughter has her Master's, and my son is completing his senior year of college.

My point is, one gets busy in life; there's always going to be something to do, someplace to go, people to meet. But, at the end of the day, family is the most important place to be.

Community … Village … Family

Call it whatever you want. Community or village, network, tribe, family, each of us needs one. All I know is my community was most unique and blessed. Don't get me wrong, it had/s its challenges, but we became stronger and shared our experiences with others. I suppose you could say, we were/are in the Service Industry.

My mother and father were raised in Washington, D. C. Both grandfathers were physicians and grandmothers, each of whom, earned their Master's, working in schools. One was the first Black woman to move into her Condo Complex, while the other boarded a wagon, fighting for a woman's right to vote.

This community ALWAYS rallied around the individual, needing assistance. No matter the situation: love, support, or encouragement, family members stepped in with a call, a knock at the door, even a flight across the country. Today, with the growth in technology, add texts, video chats, and instant messages to the list.

Children need guidance, which could come from parents, teachers, family, friends, clergy, counselors, ... We must provide opportunities for children to understand what it means to care, be gracious, proper, polite, and pleasant. And even when angry (us or them), we must model behaviors we wish them to emulate. Further, remember to guide children while managing destructive feelings.

Remember, they, too, are human and may not have the capacity to place their emotions in appropriate places. Communities, the Village, must teach them right from wrong, share good and bad, happy and sad. Be honest with them and yourself. The path is not always smooth. But, be consistent.

How do you know when *the message* has been received? When they return the gift of care and consideration to you. I experienced this recently with my adult children. I asked, "How did you turn out so wonderful, so caring?"

They responded, *"You showed us how."*

Continue Having Fun!

◇◇

Wrinkles only go where smiles have been. ~ Jimmy Buffett

I'm not certain who said it, but wrinkles mean you've laughed; grey hair means you've cared; and scars mean you've lived! People manifest things in their lives through internal and external energies, power - whatever you may wish to call "it". Where we focus those energies becomes a condition of our lives and how we choose to live. Often, expressions of these circumstances settle on our faces and attitudes.

These circumstances could be trends and fads, which seem to affect our daily decisions. Be mindful and aware of them but do not change who you are or how you dress. Suggestions of changing our thoughts and actions are prompted by the media, preparing us for the newest wave of fashion, technology, political decision, ... Just be ready for them.

Develop positive thinking practices; eliminate that which is not essential; smile, laugh, don't sweat the small stuff. Moreover, be kind to yourself. As *you* speak to *yourself,* say kind things. After all, you speak to yourself more than anyone else does. Right?

I saw a quote from tinybudda.com, which made me ponder my daily choices and obligations.

My To Do List for Today: *count my blessings,*

practice kindness, let go of what I can't control,

listen to my heart,

be productive yet calm, just breathe.

True wrinkles appear as one ages and can increase because of exposure to sun and dry skin. But, think of the wonders of those history tellers. Smiles are contagious. Are you a carrier?

Only floss the teeth you want. ~Gram

As you know if do not brush your teeth, you could suffer tooth decay or loss, bad breath, even pneumonia. According to Beth Orenstein (2012), a writer for Everyday Health, "If you want to minimize your risk of infection and also enhance your overall health, follow these basic *personal hygiene* habits: Bathe regularly. Wash your body and your hair often. Trim your nails. Brush and floss. Wash your hands. Sleep tight" (para. 1). Personal hygiene should be habit. We learn it when we are young and must continue as we age. If we do not take care of ourselves, hopefully someone else will.

The lack of personal hygiene signals a few concerns: lack of intent, unwillingness, loneliness, dementia, ... The effects of poor personal care can cause to health issues, some of which cannot be corrected. This holds most true with the aging and homeless populations. Additionally, the matter is critical to food handlers, after using the restroom. Too many people in the latter category do not feel the necessity to wash after evacuating, defecating, no. 1 or 2, whatever terminology you wish to use.

Let's take Mary Mallon, better known as "Typhoid Mary". Long story made short. Mallon, employed as a cook, did not believe washing her hands before meal preparation was necessary, as her hands were not dirty. As a consequence, many people for whom she cooked fell ill; three died (Soper, 1907).

As we age, we may need someone to assist. Start little people early, encourage family and friends around you (if they are a bit lax about it), help someone who is elderly or disabled. Their life could depend upon it.

Mistakes - the big IT.

◇◇◇◇◇◇◇◇◇◇◇◇◇◇◇◇◇◇◇◇◇◇◇◇◇◇◇◇

A man should never be ashamed to own he has been in the wrong, which is but saying... that he is wiser today than he was yesterday. -Alexander Pope

Each of us makes mistakes. What we take away from them is crucial. Were you ever told not to touch something hot? And, you did anyway and wind up with a blister? Waste material? Did you measure once then cut? Did you ever hit a ball, and it end up someplace it wasn't supposed to, like someone's window? Ever assemble a chair and have parts leftover?

Mistakes are caused by poor choices, such as texting while driving, disregarding rules, which produce negative consequences such as an accident. You know it is bad, which makes it a mistake.

Do not try to justify your mistake or blame someone else for it. Admit you made it. OWN IT! Then, begin to learn from it. The biggest mistake you can make is not learning from it.

Sometimes mistakes may involve healthcare, the law, family, friends, teachers. Whatever the mistake is you may want to take time to assess it; make sure it doesn't happen again. Perhaps this is a calling, giving you a chance to make things right, to become a better person.

Expectations

◇◇◇◇◇◇◇◇◇◇◇◇◇◇◇◇◇◇◇◇◇◇◇

"Expect the best, prepare for the worst and be prepared to be surprised."

~ Denis Waitley

Treat others the way you wish to be treated. We expect people to be open and honest with their intentions, dictating just how we want them to be. Well, you cannot!

We hold assumptions of others: how they should act, like leaving the toilet seat up, squeezing the toothpaste in the middle not the end, placing the roll of toilet paper so it unfolds from the top not from the bottom. These expectations affect our relationships.

When I was five, I vividly remember a family walk. My father and I walked together, and I tried to walk on the outside. Oh no! "Men walk on the outside; ladies walk on the inside." He explained gentlemen, particularly in this family, have traditions we express towards women:

1. A man stands when a woman walks in the room;
2. He walks on the outside, closest to the street (so she does not get splashed);
3. He opens the door for her;
4. He pulls out her chair;
5. He sits after she sits.

So many traditions have died. Though many women state they can do for themselves, and yes, I am one of them. But give me a man who believes in Chivalry, and I am in heaven.

Be careful to hold expectations of others too high. You may become disappointed, as your ideals may be unrealistic. Think about the Buddhist philosophy, "which refers to the 'waiting mind' to denote the suffering people do to themselves" (Delgado, 2018, para. 7), having preconceived notions and unreasonable expectations. Further, some may believe you to be high maintenance, ill-tempered, or simply a pain. Expect more from yourself. This is a beginning.

Invasion of the body snatchers!

Difficulty sleeping? Night sweats? Cold one minute, hot the next? Do you do a striptease without music? Decreased libido? Weight gain? Irregular heartbeat? Welcome to Menopause!

A couple of girlfriends and I got together to discuss this physiological craze of ours; the one that people call us crazy and possibly possessed. Well, we can't help it. When the menopause spirit catches you, you fall down, hiss, snarl, cry, strip. It's an outta body experience like no other. You feel like Reagan in the *Poltergeist*.

The sensation of watching yourself from outside your body is bewildering; the experience consumes you physically and mentally. Each symptom affects women differently so strap yourself in for an incredible ride. Tell your family, sorry and give them seatbelts, too. It's not your fault. The end of an era is rounding the corner. Well, in a few years!

Some things you can do are seek advice from a Healthcare Provider regarding hormone replacement. Look into herbal remedies - seek professional advice, first. Make certain you are healthy and no contraindications with current meds occur. Exercise. Aromatherapy. Consider changing your diet.

Be good to yourself. Be patient with yourself. Ask for help. *"It"* won't last forever.

Many hands make light work!

*"Success is not measured by what you accomplish, but by the opposition
you have encountered, and the courage with which you have maintained
the struggle against overwhelming odds." — Orison Swett Marden*

I could not do what I do without the assistance and cooperation of others. Sometimes, there's a bit of tugging, but in the end, what the "team" and I accomplished was worth the struggle. For each person, the struggle, though real, is measured quite differently.

Often, people who we admire most are those who struggled, searching for causes and cures. These people knew defeat, suffered, lost, leaving an immense legacy so bold and significant, we, the followers, cannot help but to continue a working for in what they believed. Mother Teresa said, "You can do what I cannot do, I can do what you cannot do. Together, we can do great things".

Any movement takes commitment. With a group working together, advancing a shared cause, the task at hand stands a better chance of completion. Sharing the wealth of achievement is priceless.

Good teams become great ones when the members trust each other
enough to surrender the me for the we. ~ Phil Jackson

Minnie's Pearl's

My grandmother's given name was Minnie; we called her Nanny. A regal woman, with grand stature, raised four children ages five to nine, after the untimely passing of her husband in 1950. She always had an appropriate quote for any situation. "Water seeks its level." Don't guild the Lilly." "This too shall pass." "Many hands make light work."

When she arrived at our home, she's settle at the Grand Piano, position herself erect, lift her hands, as though they were on air, and begin to play.

Her insight on matters of life, education, family, and not necessarily in that order, were acquired through experience and patience. When she lost my grandfather, because of a car accident, she never complained, according to Mother. She marched forward mastering an art of conversation, written and oral, sending each child to college.

I do not have all of Nanny's sayings but am on the hunt. Should your grandparent have sayings or stories, catch each word, documenting them to pass from generation to generation.

Caregivers

⬥⬥⬥⬥⬥⬥⬥⬥⬥⬥⬥⬥⬥⬥⬥⬥⬥⬥⬥⬥⬥

If there is anything I've learned over the years, Caregivers, while they strive to provide "comfort and wellbeing" (Aging.Care.com, 2018, para. 1) for others, do a poor job of giving care to themselves. They are "overextended physically, mentally, and even financially" (para. 1).

"Your" health and happiness are essential. After all, how can you give care to someone if you neglect yours? Hum. Let's think about that. According to AgingCare.com (2018), signs of Caregiver Burnout may include strange eating habits, insomnia, weak immune system, exhaustion, anger, anxiety, and more. A habit takes 21-days to become a behavior. If you have been caring for someone for a few weeks or even years, "you" may be experiencing some of these symptoms. So, let's get that behavior adjusted!

Consider a few tips. Remember, Caregivers are only HUMAN. Nothing more, nothing less. Take a break. Say no to requests. Set realistic goals. Make lists. Exercise. Get stand-in assistance. Get regular check-ups. Remember to laugh.

One of the things I learned working with veterans is we take care of those who were carried off the field. We must also care for those who did the carrying.

The break between birth & death

A Rotary Member read Linda Ellis' *The Dash,* which inspired me think a great deal about my life.

Ever blessed to have been born into my family. This family has such a rich history on both paternal and maternal sides; the challenge is enough to be a relative. We have physicians, teachers, historians, veterans, astronauts, inventors, slaves, and more. Each person holds a special story. Some unusual; some life-changing. Each person accomplished a goal (some finished; others did not), leaving his or her community a legacy upon which he or she could be remembered.

Ellis' poem also reminded me how we treat each other, what we say (or don't day) to one another, setting the wheels in motion for an event. Timeouts are very good to reset or reframe our thoughts. Active listening and thinking before we respond are essential tools for communication. If we fly off the hand or are quick to anger, people may remember us as the ones with short fuses. But, if we take the time to ponder what we would like to say, be orderly about it, slowing our thoughts, we may succeed without causing chaos.

I often thought about what people might say during my eulogy. Adjectives that come to mind are family-lover, stubborn, persnickety, exasperating, busy, ... My goal is to treat others with respect and to learn from them. I know a lot but not everything. So, just before time comes to meet your Maker, ask yourself, "Did I love, give, listen, hear, take, share..." Just what did you do between the first day and last? Whatever I did, or for that matter, continue to do, my family will always know they were first.

References

Bach, R. (1970). Jonathan Livingston Seagull. R. Munson (Ed.). London, England: MacMillian.

Brainyquotes. (n. d.a). Stephen Covey Quotes. Retrieved from https://www.brainyquote.com/authors/stephen_covey

Brainyquotes. (n. d.b) Stephen Covey Quotes. Retrieved from https://docs.google.com/document/d/1iXMS3foPWzJhA1Ft_FRiTipgOR0_yd6jYoT9oVJIGYs/edit

Brownson, J. (2016, 26 May). Can't we all just get along? Retrieved from https://www.huffingtonpost.com/jenna-brownson/cant-we-all-just-get-alon_3_b_10150704.html

Delgado, J. (2018, 29 June). The problem of expecting the others to act like you. Retrieved from https://psychology-spot.com/excessive-expectations/

DeMeyers, J. (2015, 15 September). 7 scientific reasons you always feel like you don't have enough time. Retrieved from https://www.inc.com/jayson-demers/7-scientific-reasons-you-always-feel-like-you-don-t-have-enough-time.html

Gartland, M. (2012). In three words: What does a good book represent? Retrieved from http://winningedits.com/define-a-good-book/

Jenkins, B. (2016, 4 October). Health is a gift, not a possession. Retrieved from https://www.thegospelcoalition.org/article/health-is-gift-not-possession/

Julia. (2011). Pasta is not originally from Italy. Retrieved from http://www.todayifoundout.com/index.php/2011/06/pasta-is-not-originally-from-italy/

Keierkeber, M. (2018). As Low-Income, Minority Schools see fewer resources, Civil Rights Commission calls on Congress to act. Retrieved from https://www.the74million.org/as-low-income-minority-schools-see-fewer-resources-civil-rights-commission-calls-on-congress-to-act/

Kennelly, S. (2012, 2 July). A scientific reason to stop and smell the roses. Retrieved from https://greatergood.berkeley.edu/article/item/a_scientific_reason_to_stop_and_smell_the_roses

Orenstein, B. (2012, 20 May). A guide to good personal hygiene. Retrieved from https://www.everydayhealth.com/healthy-living/guide-to-good-hygiene.aspx

Soper, G. (1907, 15 June). Mary Mallon (Typhoid Mary). *Am J Public Health Nations Health. American Public Health Association.* 29 (1): 66–8. doi:10.2105/AJPH.29.1.66.

U. S. Army Center of Military History. (n. d.). Oaths of enlistment and oaths of office.

Retrieved from https://history.army.mil/html/faq/oaths.html

Vilhauer, J. (2015, 19 April). 3 simple steps to control anger and frustration with others. Retrieved from https://www.google.com/amp/s/www.psychologytoday.com/us/blog/living-forward/201504/3-simple-steps-control-anger-and-frustration-others%3famp

About the Author

Dr. Kelly Price Noble is the Principal of KAPN Consulting: Innovative Solutions, LLC, *connecting people to people.* She is also the Program Chair, West District, for the College of Health Professions, School of Health Services Administration at University of Phoenix.

At the VA San Diego Healthcare System, she was assigned to the Spinal Cord Injury Center, as a Clinical Researcher. Previous to that, she was the Executive Director of Cal-Diego Paralyzed Veterans Association and the President of the Paralyzed Veterans of America's Association of Chapter Executive Directors, working with 34 Chapters across the nation.

Dr. Price Noble graduated from Mount Holyoke College with a B. A. in English, French, and Third World Relations. She earned a Master's Certificate from San Diego State University in Community Economic Development, a

M.A. from the University of Phoenix in Organizational Management, and a Doctorate in Health Administration from University of Phoenix.

She has more than 25 years in Public Relations, Television, and Sales experience and was an Emmy Nominee for Gallaudet University's *Fantastic*, a television program geared toward deaf and hard of hearing children.

For more than a decade, she was affiliated with the United States Navy, as a member of the Navy Wifeline Association and several Navy Spouse Clubs around the globe, including Agana, Guam and Rota, Spain. She received formal training as Casualty Assistance Calls Officer (CACO) and provided support to base activities in conjunction with Fairconron One & Two.

She is married with two adult children.